FEELINGS
1 Sadness

Tamra B. Orr

CHERRY
LAKE
Publishing

Published in the United States of America
by Cherry Lake Publishing
Ann Arbor, Michigan
www.cherrylakepublishing.com

Reading Adviser: Marla Conn MS, Ed., Literacy specialist, Read-Ability, Inc.

Photo Credits: © Happy Together/Shutterstock Images, cover, 1; © Daniel Jedzura/Shutterstock Images, 4; © Monkey Business Images/Shutterstock Images, 6; © wavebreakmedia/Shutterstock Images, 8; © Patrick Foto/Shutterstock Images, 10; © parinyabinsuk/Shutterstock Images, 12; © Tanya Little/Shutterstock Images, 14; © ZouZou/Shutterstock Images, 16; © v.schlichting/Shutterstock Images, 18; © Juanmonino/iStock Images, 20

Library of Congress Cataloging-in-Publication Data
Names: Orr, Tamra, author.
   Title: Sadness / Tamra B. Orr.
Description: Ann Arbor : Cherry Lake Publishing, 2016. | Series: Feelings | Audience: K to Grade 3. | Includes bibliographical references and index.
Identifiers: LCCN 2015048116| ISBN 9781634710459 (hardcover) | ISBN 9781634711449 (pdf) | ISBN 9781634712439 (pbk.) | ISBN 9781634713429 (ebook)
Subjects: LCSH: Sadness—Juvenile literature.
Classification: LCC BF575.S23 O77 2016 | DDC 152.4—dc23
LC record available at http://lccn.loc.gov/2015048116

Cherry Lake Publishing would like to acknowledge the work of The Partnership for 21st Century Learning. Please visit www.p21.org for more information.

Printed in the United States of America
Corporate Graphics

Table of Contents

Why do you think this boy
is sad?

Sadness

I feel so sad.

My best friend is moving away.

I lost my smile. I only have a **frown**.

Big Tears

I am sad. My eyes fill up with **tears**.

The tears get bigger and bigger.

At last, they fall and run down my face.

A Good Cry

Mom says it is okay to cry when I'm sad.

My face gets wet and red.

Later, I feel better inside.

How can you tell this boy is sad?

Finding Happiness

I cried a lot the day my friend moved.

I was so sad.

A week later, a **letter** was in my **mailbox**. It was from my friend.

I opened it. Oh, look! There is my smile again.

Find Out More

Griffin, Jennifer. *The Feeling Bag*. Mustang, OK: Tate Publishing, 2010.

Mundy, Linus. *Being Sad When Someone Dies: A Book About Grief*. St. Meinrad, IN: Abbey Press, 2012.

Glossary

frown (FROUN) a shape of the mouth that shows unhappiness
letter (LET-ur) a printed message from someone
mailbox (MAYL-bahks) a box outside a house or apartment for putting letters and packages in
tears (TEERZ) salty liquid that comes out of your eyes when you are sad

Home and School Connection

Use this list of words from the book to help your child become a better reader. Word games and writing activities can help beginning readers reinforce literacy skills.

again	feel	look	says
and	fill	lost	smile
away	friend	mailbox	tears
best	from	mom	the
better	frown	moved	there
bigger	get	moving	they
cried	gets	my	was
cry	have	okay	week
day	inside	only	wet
down	last	opened	when
eyes	late	red	with
face	later	run	
fall	letter	sad	

Index

About the Author

Tamra Orr has written more than 400 books for young people. The only thing she loves more than writing books is reading them. She lives in beautiful Portland, Oregon, with her husband, four children, dog, and cat. She admits that a good cry now and then makes her feel much better about everything.